A Let's-Read-and-Find-Out Book™

What Happens to a Hamburger

By Paul Showers

Illustrated by Anne Rockwell

Revised Edition

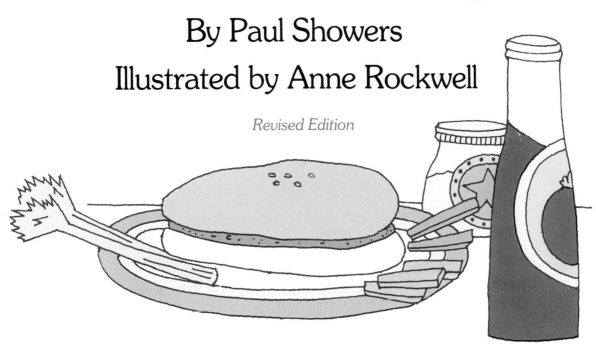

HarperTrophy

A Division of HarperCollins*Publishers*

Library of Congress Cataloging-in-Publication Data
Showers, Paul.
  What happens to a hamburger.

  (A Harper trophy book)
  (Let's-read-and-find-out books)
  Summary: Explains the processes by which a hamburger
and other foods are used to make energy, strong bones,
and solid muscles as they pass through all the parts
of the digestive system.
  1. Digestive—Juvenile literature. [1. Digestion.
2. Digestive system] I. Rockwell, Anne F., ill.
II. Title. III. Series.
QP145.S49   1985b   612′.3   84-45343
ISBN 0-06-445013-9 (pbk.)   84-48784

Published in hardcover by HarperCollins Publishers.
First Harper Trophy edition, 1985.

What Happens to a Hamburger

I like to eat.

I like bread and pears and celery. I like carrots and chicken and potatoes and hamburgers. I like orange juice and milk and tomato juice.

What do you like?

Good food makes you strong and healthy. It gives you energy and helps you grow.

Your body uses food in different ways. It uses some kinds of food to make strong bones and hard teeth. It turns other food into solid muscles. It uses some of the food you eat to keep you warm.

Before your body can do these things, it has to change the food. Solid foods like hamburgers and potatoes have to be changed into liquids. Liquids like milk and orange juice have to be changed, too.

When you change the food you eat, you are digesting it.

Put two lumps of sugar in an empty glass. Take a wooden spoon and pound the lumps with the handle. Pound them until they are broken up into powder. Now pour some water in the glass and stir. Keep stirring until the sugar powder has disappeared.

Take a sip of the water. Can you taste the sugar? The
sugar has disappeared, but it is still there. It has broken
up into millions of tiny pieces. Your eye cannot see them,
but your tongue can taste them.

When you digest your food, you break it up into millions of very tiny pieces. You start to do this as soon as you take a bite to eat. Digestion begins in your mouth when you chew. You break up the food with your teeth.

Get a piece of raw carrot and a plate. Take a bite of carrot and chew it ten times. Spit the carrot out onto the edge of the plate. Take another bite. Chew it thirty times. Spit out that mouthful on the other side of the plate. Can you see the difference?

The longer you chew food, the smaller the pieces will be.

13

Something else helps to break up the food in your mouth. It is a fluid. Some people call it spit. Its correct name is saliva.

Whenever you take a bite of food, saliva pours into your mouth. You say your mouth is watering. Saliva comes from small glands in your cheeks and under your tongue.

little openings
tongue
salivary glands

Sometimes saliva pours into your mouth even before you take a bite. The smell of food will start it. Take a good sniff of a box of chocolates. Sniff a jar of pickles. What other kinds of food make your mouth water?

After you have chewed your food, you swallow it. Your epiglottis closes. It is a door that keeps food from going into your lungs. Your throat squeezes together when you swallow. It pushes the food down into your esophagus. Another name for esophagus is gullet.

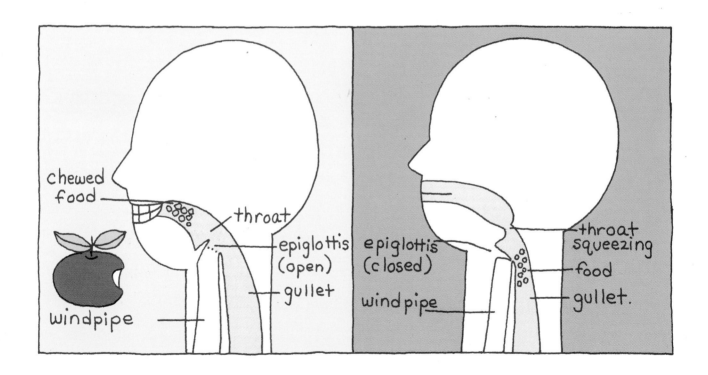

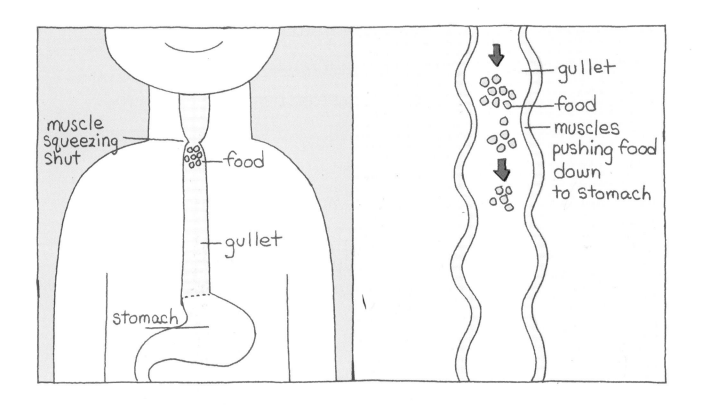

Your gullet is a tube that leads from the back of your mouth to your stomach. There are muscles in your gullet that squeeze together. They push food into your stomach.

Your stomach is a tube like your gullet. But there is a difference. Your stomach can stretch like a balloon. When you eat, your stomach stretches to hold the food.

After you swallow your meal, your stomach closes at each end. The food cannot get out. The muscles begin to squeeze. The food is mashed and stirred together.

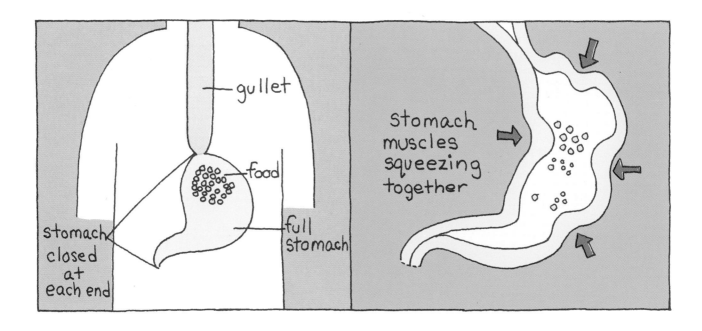

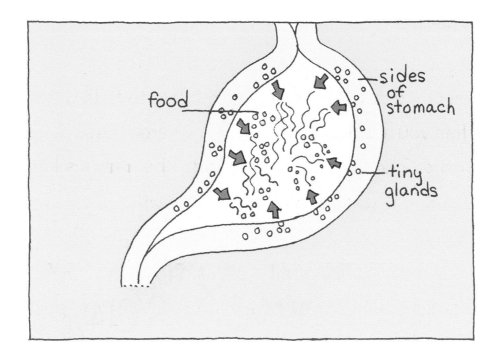

Your stomach has fluids in it like the saliva in your mouth. They are called digestive fluids. They pour in from tiny glands in the sides of the stomach. The digestive fluids help to break the food up into smaller and smaller pieces.

Food stays in your stomach for several hours. Some kinds of food stay only about two hours. Other kinds stay longer. The food stays until all the lumps have been broken up. It is like a thick soup now. It is made of millions and millions of tiny pieces.

But digestion has just begun. The tiny pieces must be made even smaller. This happens in the intestines.

There are two intestines in your body—the small intestine and the large intestine. They are really one single, long tube. This tube is coiled up inside you like a pile of heavy rope. It is about twenty-one feet long.

Most of the tube is narrow and is called the small intestine. The last four or five feet of the tube are much bigger around. This part is called the large intestine.

THE DIGESTIVE SYSTEM

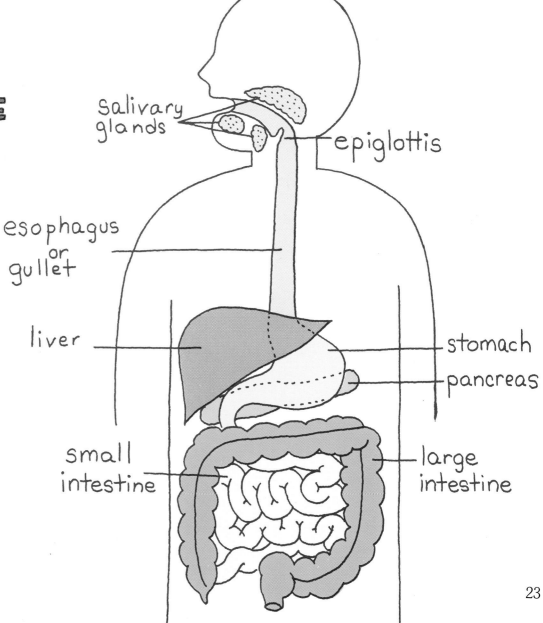

salivary glands

epiglottis

esophagus or gullet

liver

stomach

pancreas

small intestine

large intestine

The soupy food is squeezed into the small intestine from the stomach. Digestive fluids from the liver and pancreas are mixed with the food in the small intestine. These fluids break the food up into very tiny pieces called molecules. Molecules are so small you cannot see them without a special microscope.

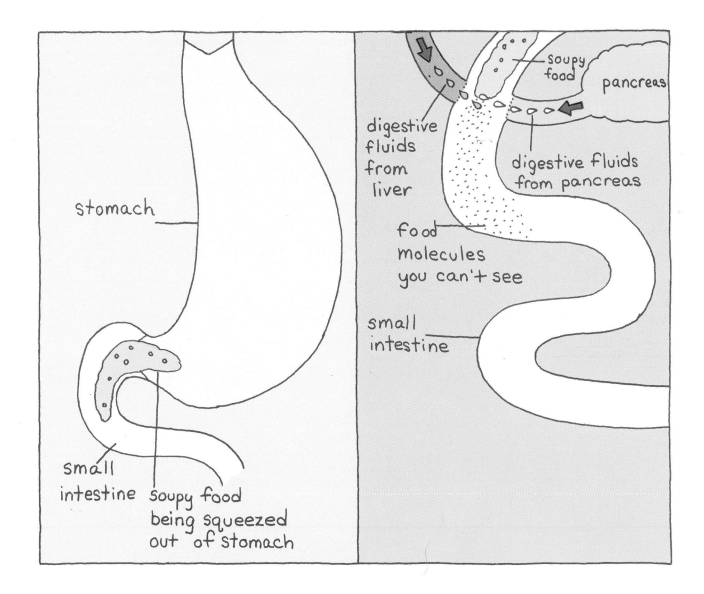

stomach

small
intestine

soupy food
being squeezed
out of stomach

digestive
fluids
from
liver

digestive fluids
from pancreas

soupy
food

pancreas

food
molecules
you can't see

small
intestine

The food molecules pass into tiny blood and lymph vessels in the walls of the small intestine. They move into your blood. Then your blood carries them to every part of your body.

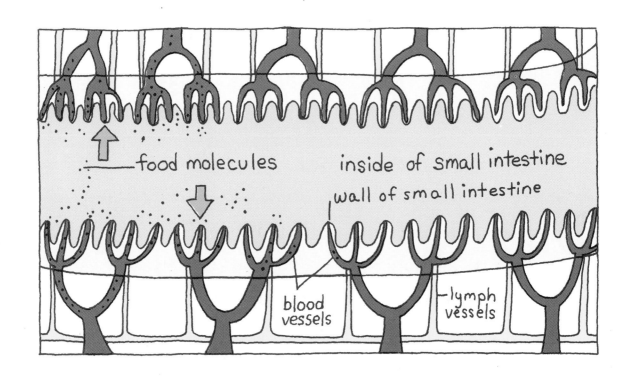

food molecules

inside of small intestine

wall of small intestine

blood vessels

lymph vessels

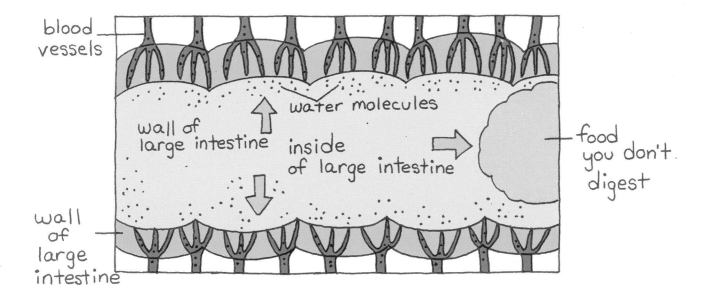

blood vessels

wall of large intestine

water molecules

inside of large intestine

food you don't digest

wall of large intestine

The part of the food that is not digested in the small intestine is squeezed into the large intestine. From here water molecules pass into the bloodstream.

Your body cannot use all of the food you eat. The food it cannot use is stored in the large intestine. You get rid of the unused food when you go to the toilet.

In the morning you may eat scrambled eggs or cereal. You may drink orange juice or hot chocolate. In a few hours, your body has digested the food. Then your blood begins to carry the tiny food molecules...

...to your muscles to make them stronger,

...to your bones and teeth to make them harder,

...to every part of your body to give you energy and help you grow.